THE

# INDESTRUCTIBLE

# SEED

## BOB HOSKINS

---

"Your word, O LORD, is eternal;
it stands firm in the heavens."
(Psalm 119:89)

"Other seeds fell into the good soil and as they grew
up and increased, they yielded a crop and produced
thirty, sixty, and a hundredfold."
(Mark 4:8)

"The Bible has survived the hatred of its enemies and the
ignorance of its friends."
—Anonymous

# Special Update
## By Rob Hoskins

September 1 is usually one of the most joyful days in Russia. It is the first day of school, and they make a big celebration out of it. The children don't go to school alone that day, but often parents and grandparents come, too. For first graders it's especially significant, because their first day of school is seen as a rite of passage: they're on their way! The whole school is decorated with balloons and flowers, and the first-graders each receive a flower as they parade into the school building, first in line, ahead of all the other children.

On September 1, 2004, the first graders in Beslan, Russia, were just leading the parade into their school with all the happy families watching and the other children set to follow — when a truck barreled through the gates and 30 masked men and women with guns piled out. At first, the children thought it was a prank, maybe something their teachers planned for a joke or some kind of fireworks display ... but when the terrorists gunned down a teacher and ordered everyone else into the gym, they realized it was deadly serious.

You saw the story unfold on the news and read about it in the newspaper. Some terrorists were already in the school, so about 60 Islamic radicals held hostage over 600 people in the tiny school gym. They denied the youngsters water — by their second day of captivity, the little ones were drinking their own urine. I can't understand that kind of hatred, bitterness and evil. It is completely demonic.

They tell me one of the terrorists didn't believe in torturing the children. She, herself, had a bomb strapped to her, when she confronted the terrorist leader to plead for mercy for the youngsters. He told her to meet him in an upstairs room to discuss her issues, and when she did, he simply detonated the bomb, killing her, then asked the others, "Does anyone else have questions?"

The killing didn't end there. I wish I could say that it did. After three days as the government attempted a rescue effort, the terrorists responded with explosives and gunfire, the roof of the gym caved in, and so many young lives were lost. There's still not an adequate death count. The government says 320 children, teachers and parents perished, but in Beslan they say the toll was much higher.

Just days later, I arrived in Russia for a previously scheduled missions visit. I've come through the Moscow airport dozens of times before, and the process is always the same:

You go through passport control, get your luggage, fill out a customs form, go through customs. When you come out of customs there is always a crowd of people you have to work your way through to find the person you are meeting. But this day in September as I came through customs, there was no jam packed crowd. There were about 300 people looking up at the television, and they were weeping. I arrived at a nation that had been so dramatically changed.

Beslan was their September 11th. Try to remember what 9/11 was for you. For days, time was suspended. It dramatically changed us as a nation. That is what Beslan was to Russia. Russia will never be the same.

The country was at a complete standstill when I arrived, and, of course, all my meetings were cancelled — for three days I was in Moscow, and all I could do was pray. The Lord revealed to me that he wanted me to go to Beslan. He said something to me then that I did not fully understand at the time: "Do you realize that I experience 9/11 every day? I see Beslan every day. I see my children go into eternity without knowledge of who I am." That is hard for us to imagine. We live in the seen, the finite, and the temporal — God sees what suffering humanity will experience without Him.

I prayed, "Lord, help me to try to see the world as You see it."

Maybe that is impossible, but the Lord told me at that time to visit Beslan, and I would experience a little of what He experiences every time a lost soul goes into eternity without Him. In Beslan, I simply wept for days. With each new friend I made, I heard a new story of horror and tragedy. It is a small town of only 33,000 people, so literally every family was touched in some way by this madness.

One young mother had accompanied her proud six-year-old boy to school that day, carrying her baby in her arms. At one point, the terrorists grew tired of hearing babies cry and commanded all mothers with babies to leave — the woman tried to leave with her baby and her little son, but they wouldn't allow it. She could leave with her baby, but she must leave her son behind. Her little boy was one of those who did not survive, and now his mother lives with that pain and guilt ... guilt because she was forced to abandon one child to save the other.

At the local church, two brothers serve as associate pastors. Between them, they had eight children at school that day. All but two were killed. The Sunday school has a regular attendance of 38 children, all taken captive in the gym, along with their Sunday School teacher. Sixteen of those children, and their teacher, were killed.

But before they went home to see Jesus, those Christian youngsters had a vital role to play. They joined together to sing, "God is so good, God is so good..." Their little voices reaffirmed their faith in their heavenly Father. Then they took the Word they had hid in their hearts, and they wrote it down on scraps of paper to pass to the other children: they copied out the Lord's prayer as a gift of comfort to their classmates.

In that darkest hour, the youngsters from children's church understood the only words that console are the words of Jesus, because they were experiencing this themselves. When you come to a living hell, there is only Jesus — the only hope, consolation, peace. The children understood where they were going, thank God there was remnant in that school.

I cried as I heard their stories. I wept until I thought I had no more tears. I couldn't sleep. I went to the cemetery where there are over 300 graves of children. Parents were just wailing, weeping. I saw an old man weeping by a grave where two bodies were side by side. He was saying, "This was my only daughter, my only grandchild."

The rubble of the school building still stands, and still today, three months after the tragedy, parents walk the shattered halls, weeping. Surviving children leave the favored toys of their dead brothers or sisters with a little note, a memorial to their lost loved ones. Some leave bottles of water open as little shrines to those who died tortured and thirsty.

For those few days, I saw the world a little bit as Jesus sees it, heart-broken and stunned at the immensity of the tragedy.

But a part of me cried out for revenge, too. Surely such great evil should not go unanswered? Maybe some of the terrorists were killed when the government forces moved in, and maybe Russian and international authorities will track down those who escaped ... but it's not enough to catch the human perpetrators of this crime, because they aren't the ones responsible for it, ultimately.

This kind of evil is only dreamed up in the heart of hell, and it is only inspired by Satan and his demons. If we want true revenge, if we want to make a faithful response against the real architect of this madness, then we need to strike right at the originator of it, the devil himself.

And do you know what the enemy hates more than anything else? He doesn't like it when the innocent are protected. He doesn't like it when governments respond and bring offenders to justice. But do you know what he really hates? He hates when we save people from his eternal unseen kingdom of everlasting suffering. He hates it more than if we were able to go into that school and save every one of those children from death. He hates it far more when a child accepts Jesus and escapes the threat of eternal damnation.

So if we want our real revenge on Satan, then what we need to do is bring children to Jesus. I made a pledge in that cemetery in Beslan. There will not be a town or village in Russia, in Central Asia that does not know that Jesus is the Savior. I told the devil: "I pledge to you that until I die, that in every town, village, and hamlet the Word of the Lord will go forth and reach every child in the former Soviet Union. Hear me enemy. What you intended for evil, the church through God's power will use for good."

That is our retribution. That is our response. And there is nothing the devil hates worse than that — unless it would be to expand that pledge from "across the former Soviet Union" to "around the whole world." In fact, that is our pledge at the Book of Hope ministry: *God's Word. Every Child!* I have a real burden for Russia and the former USSR, but at the same time, we are reaching children and youth with the life-transforming Word of God on every continent! And our pledge is not to stop until every child and youth has received the Word.

In the pages of this book, my father shares His heart and the vision God gave us to take His Word to all the children and youth of the world. You will discover that truth, and the power which goes with the Word, wherever it goes. As you read, keep in mind, when you give the Word of God to the children of the world, you are having your revenge on the devil ... not just for Beslan, but for 9/11 and for every evil that he has perpetrated on us since Adam and Eve. Because the thing he hates most is when another lost soul surrenders to the love of Jesus.

# Table *of* Contents

# Preface

## God's Word.
## Every Child.

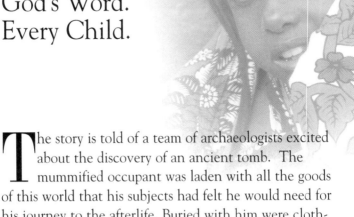

The story is told of a team of archaeologists excited about the discovery of an ancient tomb. The mummified occupant was laden with all the goods of this world that his subjects had felt he would need for his journey to the afterlife. Buried with him were clothing, tools, plates and dishes, food, even servants and pets who had been put to death so they could continue to serve the king in the life to come.

Also found among the provisions for the afterlife were implements for farming, and packets of seeds. An expert in ancient flora was asked to identify the various seeds, and found that some were actually the seeds of plants that had long been extinct. For centuries, the seeds of these all-but-forgotten plants had been tucked away in the tomb with the dead king. When the herb expert planted them in modern soil and watered them, even after all the years, the seeds sprouted and introduced the extinct plant to a whole new world!

The Word of God is like those seeds, an indestructible force that — no matter how its enemies may try to bury it, no matter how its opponents may declare it extinct — blossoms into brand-new life for those who believe. The Psalmist declared, *"Your word, O Lord, is eternal; it stands firm in the heavens"* (Psalm 119:89). The Word of God is the indestructible seed that brings salvation and eternal life.

At the *Book of Hope* ministry, we believe this powerful seed can be planted in every young person, all around the world, over the next several years. Our vision: *God's Word. Every Child.*

In the pages of this book, you will discover the eternal power of the Word, and how you can be part of scattering this seed to the four corners of the earth, and help hasten that day when the glory of the Lord will free the whole earth.

# Introduction
## The Indestructible Seed

*"He also said, 'This is what the kingdom of
God is like. A man scatters seed on the ground.
Night and day, whether he sleeps or gets up, the seed
sprouts and grows, though he does not know how. All
by itself the soil produces grain--first the stalk, then
the head, then the full kernel in the head. As soon as
the grain is ripe, he puts the sickle to it, because the
harvest has come.'"* (Mark 4:26-29)

*"I have for many years made it a practice to read
through the Bible once a year. My custom is to read four or
five chapters every morning after rising from my bed. It
employs about an hour of my time and seems to me the most
suitable manner of beginning the day."*

— John Quincy Adams

An outspoken agnostic named Robert Ingersoll crisscrossed the United States during the 19th century, ridiculing the Bible everywhere he went. In one of his books, *The Mistakes of Moses,* he claimed, "in 25 years ... the Bible will be a forgotten book."

I checked the main library in Miami to see how often Ingersoll's book was being checked out ... They haven't had the book for so long they don't even have a record of it. I called the three largest bookstores to see if they had copies; they didn't.

The Bible lives on and on, in spite of all the Ingersolls and other detractors who would love to see it obliterated. Why such staying power for an old book? Because the Bible is the only book through which God speaks. This book is important to God, because without it, we would be ignorant of His plan of salvation — a plan in which He invested the life of His only Son! Without the indispensable Word of God, we would know nothing

> *"The Bible lives on and on, in spite of all the ...detractors who would love to see it obliterated. Why such staying power for an old book?"*

of Bethlehem's manger or Calvary's cross. *"Faith cometh by hearing, and hearing by the Word of God,"* Paul wrote in Romans 10:17. The Bible is indispensable to salvation!

Martin Luther was a pious priest, trying by penance and pain to gain forgiveness — all to no avail. One day in a letter he exclaimed in despair, "Oh my sin, my sin, my sin!"

But then, as he read the Bible in the tower of the Wittenberg monastery, Luther suddenly and fully realized, *"the just shall live by faith"* (Romans 1:17). Luther was dramatically changed by God's Word — and he went on to change the world forever.

God's Word is indispensable and He will not let it die!

Accordingly, He has filled his Word with a power unlike anything else we see in the universe ... a power that transcends natural law, a power that transforms the destinies of men. *"Forever, O Lord, Thy Word is settled in heaven,"* Psalm 119:89 says.

Ingersoll was not the first man in history to try to destroy God's Word. Jehoiakim took a penknife to Jeremiah's inspired scroll, then cast the shredded pages into the fire. But he could not blot out God's message (Jeremiah 26:23). Voltaire boasted, "Another century and there will not be a Bible on earth." Voltaire is gone, and his books are found mostly in libraries and second-hand bookstores. But the Bible continues to gain in popularity — it's the biggest selling book of all publishing history — and Voltaire's own house is now the home of a Bible society!

The Word of God is the most powerful force in the cosmos, more powerful than governments, more powerful than any army, more powerful than nuclear energy. Jesus said of this Living Word, *"Even the Heavens and the earth will pass away, but my Word will never pass away."* This Word exists eternally.

Wherever the Bible goes, it lives and it changes lives miraculously.

The Scriptures continue to transform lives to this day — whether they are delivered on the printed page, through the Internet, on cable TV, or even the Silver Screen.

This is why we are committed to getting the Scripture to every youth, boy and girl, worldwide. Our vision: *God's Word. Every Child.*

# CHAPTER ONE

# Problems *with the* Great Commission

**"The grass withers and the flowers fall, but the word of our God stands forever."**
(Isaiah 40:8)

*"An atheist was visiting an island whose natives were once cannibals. He saw an elderly man reading a Bible and ridiculed him for reading a book 'full of myths and fables'. The native said, 'Friend be grateful we believe this book, otherwise we would be eating you for dinner.' The Bible does indeed change people!"*

— Unknown

# Problems *with the* Great Commission

Let's face it: In some ways, the Great Commission sounds like a joke. Jesus commanded us to go into all the world and take His message of salvation to every person. But there are now more than six billion people on this globe! Surely He was joking! Or at least speaking figuratively!

But no, Jesus was speaking quite literally.

Still, how can it happen? If we had begun winning converts at the rate of 1 per minute on the very day Jesus arose, we would have won only one billion souls from then until today. Obviously not fast enough!

Suppose we could win 3,000 souls a day, as the disciples did at Pentecost. How long would it take to win the six billion people alive today? The answer: 5,479 years!

If Abraham had won 3,000 converts every day and his descendants had continued to do so, it would still take us until A.D. 3000 to evangelize *just the people living on the earth in the year 2000.*

Right now there are more than 3 billion people on this planet untouched by the Gospel of Jesus Christ. Yet Christ said clearly, go to *all* the world. No, it is not presumptuous to believe that it can be done. It must be done! It will be done! If it were truly impossible, Jesus would never have commanded us to do it.

It is not impossible to see the world saturated with God's Word. It is possible because we have been commanded, and we are compelled to go, to work, to send the Word of God. It is possible because we have been promised the support and power of God's Holy Spirit in the accomplishment of the goal.

But obeying Jesus' command will never be accomplished by ordinary methods. It will never be accomplished by just hoping, that's for sure. It will only be done when the Church rolls up its sleeves and says, "With God's anointing, we are going to finish the task. We are going to saturate our world with the glorious news of Jesus' saving grace. We are going to hasten that moment when Christ shall return."

Yes, we need missionaries, teachers, pastors, and dedicated Christians working one-on-one, face-to-face, with those who need Jesus. But the fact that there are not enough missionaries and dedicated Christians makes the winning of the world with the one-on-one evangelism alone all but impossible.

Did you know that 685 children starve to death

every *hour?* That's six million children per year. Billions more — children and adults — are starving spiritually, choking on the lies they're fed by anti-God forces.

How many of those dying today from malnutrition, while you're reading this book, will die also of spiritual hunger, never having been told about Jesus Christ?

And what will you do about all those born as you turn these pages?

Thank God, there is an answer that is doable for you and me, today.

God's written Word has proven powerful in evangelism and the establishment of God's Kingdom, according to His promise in Isaiah 55:11. *"So shall my word be that goes out from my mouth; it shall not return to me empty, but it shall accomplish that which I purpose, and shall succeed in the thing for which I sent it."*

The Word is the Way — the indestructible seed — that goes even where missionaries cannot go, and reaches millions who may never even have heard a Christian speak a single sentence.

It reaches people like Nassi.

Some years ago there was a paper shortage in Teheran, the capital of Iran. A young Muslim named Nassi happened to be going to the market to buy cheese. The vendor, without regular food-wrapping paper, wrapped the cheese in a printed page. The paper caught Nassi's eye. At home, he carefully unwrapped the cheese and pressed out the stained page.

Nassi began reading the words, then showed the paper to his father, who suspected — rightly — that it had come from a Christian Bible. He warned his son against reading it, or any other pages like it. But the young man was thoroughly captivated by the message he had stumbled upon.

*"Soon the young man had quite a collection of Bible pages, all of which he kept hidden from his father."*

The next day, Nassi went back to the same food merchant and inquired, as discreetly as possible, about the mysterious page. The merchant told him that if he would buy something else, he could have more of the same "wrapping paper." Nassi quickly requested some figs. They were also wrapped in a printed page.

Nassi began a series of purchases: dates, then more cheese, and on and on. Soon the young man had quite a collection of Bible pages, all of which he kept hidden from his father. Naturally the pages were not in sequence, and they offered only bits and pieces of information, and Nassi was frustrated.

But he was not discouraged. He began searching until he found an entire Bible in his native Farsi language.

Within just a few weeks, Nassi was drawn to the Lord and accepted Christ as his Savior.

That is the power of the printed page! That is the hunger of the world!

*The Bible is not just so much ink on paper,* God's Word is alive and the Holy Spirit is committed to accompanying His Word wherever it goes — which often means places where missionaries can't go.

# CHAPTER TWO

# The
# Breath *of*
# Inspiration

**"Long ago I learned from your
statutes that you
established them to last
forever"** (Psalm 119:152).

*"Speaking from personal
experience, I would therefore say
that if you want to open up a new
area, the first thing to do is send
them a Bible."*

— F.C. Glass

# The
# Breath *of*
# Inspiration

More than 2,600 times in the Old Testament, and another 525 times in the New Testament, the Bible claims to be the Word of God. It is important to God that we realize the Bible's authorship! He inspired its writing, and He lives in its pages.

The word "inspired" can be traced to the verb "to breathe." The connotation is that of a flutist breathing into his instrument to produce a beautiful sound. This is how God breathed His message — through individual writers — to arrive at the inspired result.

Accepting the fact of inspiration is crucial to the future of the Church. "The biggest division between Christians is no longer between one denomination and another," said Dr. J. Sidlow Baxter, "but between those who accept the Bible as the inspired Word of God and those who do not."

If the Book is not inspired, then we're wasting our time!

Furthermore, the Bible is incorruptible. It is

inerrant forever. *"Being born again, not of corruptible seed, but of incorruptible,"* 1 Peter 1:23 declares, *"by the Word of God, which liveth and abideth forever."*

William E. Gladstone, the great English statesman, called the Bible "the impregnable rock of Holy Scriptures." And the late Dr. A.Z. Conrad so eloquently wrote:

> *Century follows century — There it stands.*
> *Empires rise and fall and are forgotten — There it stands.*
> *Dynasty succeeds dynasty — There it stands.*
> *Kings are crowned and uncrowned — There it stands.*
> *Emperors decree its extermination — There it stands.*
> *Despised and torn to pieces — There it stands.*
> *Storms of hate swirl about it — There it stands.*
> *Atheists rail against it — There it stands.*
> *Agnostics smile cynically — There it stands.*
> *Profane prayer-less punsters caricature it —*
> *        There it stands.*
> *Unbelief abandons it — There it stands.*
> *Higher critics deny its claim to inspiration —*
> *        There it stands.*
> *Thunderbolts of wrath smite it — There it stands.*
> *An anvil that has broke a million hammers —*
> *        There it stands.*
> *The flames are kindled about it — There it stands.*
> *The arrows of hate are discharged against it —*
> *        There it stands.*

*Radicalism rants and raves about it — There it stands.*
*Fogs of sophistry conceal it temporarily —*
> *There it stands.*
*The tooth of time gnaws but dents it not —*
> *There it stands.*
*Infidels predict its abandonment — There it stands.*
*It is God's highway to Paradise.*
*It is the light on the pathway in the darkest night.*
*It leads businessmen to integrity and uprightness.*
*It is the great consoler in bereavement.*
*It awakens men and women opiated by sin.*
*It answers every great question of the soul.*
*It solves every great problem of life.*
*It is a fortress often attacked but never failing.*
*Its wisdom is commanding and its logic convincing.*
*Salvation is its watchword. Eternal life its goal.*
> *It punctures all pretense.*
*It is forward-looking, outward-looking, and*
> *upward-looking.*
*It outlives, outlifts, outloves, outreaches, outranks,*
> *outruns all other books.*
*Trust it, love it, obey it, and Eternal Life is yours.*

The power of the Word to stand the test of time cannot be overstated. Consider this testimony: in the Southeast Asian nation of Laos, during the final days of the French involvement there, a French missionary felt burdened to reach the tribes of the remote mountain regions. But because of communist insurgents, he couldn't reach them. One day, as he drove along a street in the capital city, he saw some men from one of the tribes he longed to reach — he recognized them by their dress.

The missionary stopped them and tried to talk to them in French, but they spoke no French. Determined, the missionary convinced them, by gestures and facial expressions, to get into his jeep and come with him.

At his home, the missionary gave the tribesmen some food, along with a French New Testament and some other Christian literature. He knew they couldn't read any of it, but the tribesmen happily took the gifts back to their mountain village.

*"There, one of the tribesmen gave the Bible to the only person in the village who could read — the witch doctor!"*

There, one of the tribesmen gave the Bible to the only person in the village who could read — the witch doctor! He had learned French at a government school years before.

A full seven years passed. The French and the communist insurgents worked out a truce. Finally, the missionary was able to visit the mountain area he had wanted to reach with the Gospel for so long. For three days he traveled, first by train, then by horseback.

There, the missionary was astonished.

The witch doctor had read the Bible and the literature, accepted Christ as his Savior, and shared his new life with others in the village. As their witch doctor, he was respected, and the villagers listened to him night after night as he read from the Scripture.

All 57 adults in the village came to accept Jesus Christ.

But the enthusiastic new believers weren't content. They determined to spread the Word to the next village. When they were finished evangelizing there, they went to the next village, and the next, and the next.

The French missionary was astounded to discover 11 remote villages where the Gospel had been preached — 748 Christian tribesmen in all!

There was not a single fancy church building, no powerful preacher, no daily television or radio program — just one French Bible and a few pieces of Christian literature. From his Word, they knew that the God who had created all things sent His Son to earth. They knew the Son of God had died in man's place and had been raised from the grave. They knew *"Whosoever believeth in him should not perish, but have everlasting life."*

Oh, the power of God's Word to bring light!

During the days I was leading the ministry of Life Publishers International, we received a call at our office from a chaplain in the Puerto Rican prison system. He described the utterly deplorable conditions there. In fact, inmates were sometimes murdered in their cells as they slept. The chaplain believed if he could get some Bibles into the hands of the prisoners, it would make a difference, and he asked if we could help. We sent him several thousand Bibles.

In less than three months, he reported to us that 750 men had given their hearts to Jesus as a result of receiving Bibles. He later sent us a list of 52 names of *former prisoners who are now going into the ministry!*

Wherever Bibles and Christian literature are introduced, the planting of churches and great spiritual blessing follow. Many authorities on church growth attribute the amazing growth of the church in Brazil and other South American countries, for example, to the strong emphasis on prior Bible distribution as a first step in church planting.

F.C. Glass, a pioneer in missionary Bible and literature distribution, says, "In dozens of places where I sold the first copies of Scriptures the people ever saw, there are strong evangelical churches today ... It was almost invariably the case where the Bible came first ... then later the preacher. *I cannot recall a single incidence where the Bible came second.*"

CHAPTER THREE

# Good News

"But the word of the Lord stands forever. And this is the word that was preached to you." (I Peter 1:25)

*"Sin will keep you from the Bible, or the Bible will keep you from sin."*

— Dwight L. Moody

# Good News

Ed Johnson is a living example of the effectiveness of God's Word.

He received an MBA from the University of Pennsylvania's Wharton School of Business, one of the most prestigious schools in America. For seven years Ed was a CPA with one of the top five accounting firms in the world. Later he moved to the Revlon Corporation, where he quickly advanced to the highest echelon of management, and was responsible for market planning in Europe, Africa, and the Middle East.

But soon the climb up the corporate ladder began to take its toll. It destroyed his home and his health, and it was quickly destroying his soul. Finally, Ed quit the company and began a search for the Truth.

For two years Ed traveled all over the world trying to find answers to his life's dilemmas. He studied the mystical Eastern religions. He read books covering every branch of philosophy.

One day, as he sat in the library of his apartment in Paris, he began to peruse the titles of his many books, thinking how little they had all helped. He had read hundreds of books, and still had not found whatever it was he was searching for.

But Ed's aunt had recently given him a copy of the *Good News for Modern Man* New Testament. Alone in his apartment, Ed began reading this book and then he read it again several times. What two years of extensive traveling, intensive searching, and much studying had failed to do, the Bible was able to do.... It gave Ed answers he had been searching for.

> "What two years of extensive traveling, intensive searching, and much studying had failed to do, the Bible was able to do...."

Knowing finally that he must give his heart and his life to Jesus Christ, but not knowing exactly how to do this, Ed began searching through his library once again to see if he could find any Christian book that might help him.

Eventually, he came upon a paperback book written

by Oral Roberts, and there on the last page of the book he found instructions for accepting Jesus as his personal Savior and praying the sinner's prayer. Ed went through the steps as instructed, and on his knees he invited Jesus into his heart. From that moment, Christ began to direct the steps of his life.

Later, Ed served as vice-president of a large literature ministry, using his talents, skills, and knowledge to help get God's message in printed form into the hands of others who are seeking the Truth as he was. Ed Johnson understands clearly the mighty power of God's Word to change lives.

Another story of how the Good News transformed a man in need:

Several years ago, a musical superstar named Barry McGuire, well known for his hit record "The Eve of Destruction," was walking along a street in California in a drunken stupor. As he stumbled along a young "Jesus person" passed him, and thrust a New Testament into Barry's hand.

Barry looked down at the book and read the title on the cover: *Good News for Modern Man.*

"Hey! I'm a modern man," he said to himself, "and I could sure use a little good news."

So he took the book home with him.

But Barry McGuire didn't read the book. It lay forgotten under his piano.

Months later, after another long period of partying and drinking, Barry noticed the book. For some reason, he felt compelled to read it. As he read, the Holy Spirit, who always accompanies God's Word wherever we send it, made Christ real to Barry McGuire. Today he's singing songs for Jesus, and has led thousands to Christ.

This is the power, the potential, of the Word of God.

That power to touch men's hearts is absolutely undeniable. Christian literature anointed by the Holy Spirit is always effective. We must use the powerful Word of God in order to fulfill Christ's injunction to reach all the world.

The power of God's Word isn't the only thing that is undeniable. The *need* for God's Word is also undeniable. Billions are without Christ. Billions have never heard or read about Jesus. These are *people*. People as countless as the stars. Eternal souls for whom Christ suffered and died.

Carl Sagan, the well known humanistic astronomer and scientist, often expressed his awe over the "billions and billions" of stars in space. And yet Sagan denied that there is a God. The vastness of God's creation did not move him.

Tragically, we Christians are, in many ways, just like the atheistic scientist. We are awed by the numbers — the billions and billions of lost souls — but we are not moved to act.

And what is our excuse?

Some say the problem is too big, there are too many people, we'll never be able to reach them all. But to say those things is to deny the power of God, and to deny the reality of what we have seen accomplished through God's Word.

We have seen God's Word turn back the tide of famine ... of drug abuse ... of Marxist ideology ... of war. We have seen the Scriptures rejuvenate the sagging spirit of the wandering refugee, and empower the struggling underground Church.

We know, firsthand, that there is no greater power on earth than the power of God's Word.

# CHAPTER FOUR

# A Vision

**"Where there is no vision
the people perish ..."**
(Proverbs 29:18)

*"The Christians who have turned
the world upside down have been
men and women with a vision
in their hearts and
the Bible in
their hands."*

— *T.B. Maston*

# A Vision

For many years, I served as President of Life Publishers, at the time one of the largest Gospel publishing houses in the world. I was so committed to the printed Word of God, and I had seen its power to save! Our ministry translated great Christian works into many languages and saw them placed into the hands of believers and non-believers around the world. We had many translations of the Bible and important study Bibles for pastors in nation after nation. We developed and produced The Full Life Study Bible, now widely known as The Fire Bible. It was a fulfilling work in every way.

Then in 1987, during a time of fasting and prayer, God showed me a vision: horrible scenes of how Satan was going to unleash the greatest spiritual attack this planet has ever known — that he was going to unleash all of his hellish powers to destroy an entire generation. I saw him specifically releasing demons to target the children and young people for destruction.

Through poverty and famine, through violence and war, through the proliferation of alcohol, drugs, and sexual permissiveness, with the accompanying diseases like AIDS, Satan would try to wipe out an entire generation. As these horrible scenes of death and carnage unfolded before me, for days I was weeping and crying, "God what are you saying? What does this mean? What am I to do?"

As I cried out to God for an answer to what this was all about, He spoke, "The only thing that overcomes lies is truth. My Word is truth. I want you to take My Word to the youth and children of the world, and you will do it through leaders."

I asked my good friend and ministry partner, Dr. Dale Berkey, to pray with me about this burden, and as he and I sought the Lord together in an intense time of prayer the message became clear: God wanted us to take His Word to the children of the world, and He would open doors through world leaders.

I knew what God meant by His Word; I knew what He meant by children; I wasn't sure what He meant by leaders. Since we were the largest publisher of Christian material in several languages, including the Spanish language, I decided to start with leaders in Spanish-speaking nations of the world. We got the names of the fifty most powerful leaders in every Spanish-speaking country, presidents, vice-presidents, heads of education and the military, and business people and I had their names embossed in gold on one of our beautiful leather Spanish study Bibles. We sent these Bibles out with a message commending God's Word as a map for their life and as a guide for their nation.

The response was incredible. Within weeks I was receiving response from leaders across the Latin world. As a result, I was a guest of the presidents of several nations, and had the chance to share with them, personally, the importance of the Word of God.

But the most remarkable response came from the country of El Salvador, where the Minister of Education wrote to thank me for the Bible and then went on to describe the horrible civil war that was tearing his nation apart. He said that it was the children that were suffering the most; their hope and their future had been stolen. He asked if it was possible for us to provide Bibles for all the children in all the schools of El Salvador.

*He said that it was the children that were suffering the most; their hope and their future had been stolen.*

Imagine my excitement! I responded immediately with a great big "yes!" not even knowing how many children there were or where I would get the Bibles to provide them.

After I had sent him my enthusiastic response, I thought to turn to my secretary and ask, "How many schoolchildren are there in El Salvador?"

It turned out there were close to one million. Maybe I should have asked that before I sent the telegram, but too late now. One million children would be counting on us to give them God's Word. So what should we give them?

We decided, if we had the one chance to take the Word of God to an entire generation, we had to give them what was most important: the Gospel — Jesus' story and Jesus' words. So we teamed up with an educational specialist to harmonize the four Gospels, so that we could tell the life story of Jesus in chronological order, with nothing repeated, but nothing left out. We came up with *El Libro de Vida*, which would become our *Book of Hope*. It told everything of Jesus' story, from his virgin birth in the stable to His teachings and miracles, to His death on the cross and glorious resurrection. We added 100 study questions at the end of the book that directed the students back into the Word, and we made sure the book had a plan of salvation that clearly told children how to accept Christ as Savior.

What happened next was a real miracle of partnership and unity among God's people in the U.S. and in El Salvador. I wrote to all of my friends and told them about this wide open door to help the children of El Salvador. I told them we could print this book and get it to the kids for just 50¢ per child.

Meanwhile a great missionary, John Bueno, was organizing the believers of El Salvador. They had agreed to receive the books when they arrived, and take them to every school across the nation.

I heard from two close friends and ministry partners, Chuck Freeman and Jim Holt. These two men (Jim has since gone on to be with the Lord) have been leaders in Light For The Lost, an organization that provides literature materials for missionaries. When they heard of this incredible opportunity they said, "Go for it! This is what LFTL is all about," and pledged $250,000 in seed money. Others responded with the additional $250,000 needed to reach every child in El Salvador.

Our El Salvadoran partners took the books in boxes and baskets, in cars and trucks, on bicycles, donkeys and even balanced on their heads, and trekked them into every school and into the hands of every schoolchild in the nation, from the largest city schools to the tiniest forgotten one-room school houses of the countryside.

I remember so vividly the story of one teacher way out in the countryside who broke down in tears when one of the brothers arrived with the books. "A gift for us?" she cried. "No one ever remembers us out here!"

Further, many of the teachers told the local volunteers, "You can't just give us this book and leave. We don't know anything about it. Why don't you tell the children what is in this book, and explain it to us?" Across El Salvador, the followers of Jesus had an opportunity to stand up in front of classroom after classroom and explain the Gospel of Jesus Christ to the students and teachers. Many times they were even able to lead the children in praying to receive Christ as Savior, right there at school.

The Bible-believing churches of El Salvador began to fill with new believers. We received report after report of children and their families, committing their lives to Christ because of God's Word in the pages of the *Book of Hope*. Soon other Spanish-speaking nations were asking for *El Libro de Vida* for their students. Word of this book's potential was racing across Latin America and the Caribbean, and even around the world. Then we should have expected it, but we didn't; a missionary from the island of Haiti called and said, "What are the chances you can get that book translated into French for Haiti?" It was amazing! When some of the French-speaking nations of Africa heard that the book might be translated into French, they immediately requested it for their schoolchildren.

My son Rob was a grown man by now, a youth pastor in California. He and his youth group were scheduled to go on a missions trip to Honduras, and I convinced him he could take the *Book of Hope* to the students of Honduras. The doors were opening to so many Spanish-speaking nations, and Honduras was one that had requested the book anyway. So Rob agreed to get his youth group involved in taking the book to the students of Honduras.

Rob and his team presented the *Book of Hope* in a high school with 17,000 students. They began reaching the students in stages, doing assembly after assembly throughout the day. The response was so overwhelming, school officials asked them to return the next day and continue until they had reached every student with God's Word.

The second day, a young man caught Rob's eye. Just yesterday, he said, he had been dissatisfied and militant, and had joined one of the radical groups that plotted to overthrow the government by violence. But then he had received the *Book of Hope* at one of the assemblies. He took it home and read it through three times! He felt some power in the pages of this book that drained him of his desire for violence and radical rebellion ... instead, he wanted to know Jesus!

Rob had the privilege of leading the young man to Jesus, right there at school. In a moment of time, the poverty, abuse and hopelessness he had lived with all his life fell away, and the Savior brought him into a new life of hope for eternity.

And this phenomenon, the *Book of Hope en español*, was really just the beginning of what God had planned.

He was guiding us to our ministry vision: *God's Word. Every Child.*

# CHAPTER FIVE

# The *Book of Hope*

## Into All The World

*"He said to them, 'Go into all the world and preach the good news to all creation.'"* **(Mark 16:15)**

*"If the choice were ever to be between the Bible without the teacher or the teacher without the Bible, I would unhesitatingly choose the former."*

— Dr. G. F. Verbeck

# The *Book of Hope*

## Into All The World

After the triumphant arrival of the *Book of Hope* in El Salvador, it became a challenge to see where we could go next with God's Word. Rob was so impacted by this vision and what he had seen in Honduras, he rapidly became more involved with the ministry.

With Rob, my friend Dale, and our staff, we began to plan for taking the *Book of Hope* to the children of the world. We discovered that if we could translate the existing *Book of Hope* into just 10 major languages, we could conceivably reach 60% of the schoolchildren of the world. With just 20 languages, we could reach nearly 90% of the world's schoolchildren.

We put all the easy languages at the top of the list: Spanish, French, Portuguese, figuring we could do those, no problem. All the tough ones went way down to the bottom of the list. One day a man who was visiting our offices looked at my list, and he said, "You're leaving out millions of children if you don't get Russian on the list."

This was the 1980's, and the Soviet Union looked like it would last another 70 years easily. The Iron Curtain seemed as firmly in place as it had ever been, and the last I had heard, it was still a serious crime to smuggle contraband literature into Russia.

I had no problem with those whom God had called to smuggle Bibles. I have had and continue to have nothing but the greatest admiration for people like Brother Andrew. But God had told us that we would go through the front door that we would reach the children through the leaders, and I saw no possible way that that would happen in Russia, at least in my lifetime.

I told the inquiring friend as much, as though the matter was closed. But a few months later, I was in prayer with some friends, and the Lord told me to put the *Book of Hope* into the Russian language. That was on Friday. On Monday, when I returned to my offices I had visitors with a shocking inquiry. A wonderful brother from Sweden who had a compassionate ministry to some of the physical needs in the Soviet Union had been given a permit to legally import fifty thousand Bibles. They said they wanted this limited distribution to be evangelistic and wanted to use the *Book of Hope*. I explained that my specific direction was to take it to children and youth, and if ever there were an opportunity to do that in Russia, I would enthusiastically participate. A few months later, they were back with an invitation to accompany them, as special guests of the Soviet government.

Stunned and thrilled, Rob and I went to Russia with these businessmen, and there we were introduced to the Minister of Education for the Russian Republic, Igor Vischepan. When he heard about the *Book of Hope*, he told me, "You're late, Mr. Hoskins. You're in a race for the souls of the next generation, and you're already losing it. The Mormons are already here. The Moonies are already here. The Hare Krishna's are already here. The Church of Satan is even here. You're late." With that, he gave me permission to bring the *Book of Hope* for every schoolchild in the Soviet Union, more than 60 million students!

By God's grace, the *Book of Hope* has now been distributed to more than 40 million students across the former USSR. The testimonies of the impact of God's Word would literally fill volumes of books.

> "*...we had 68,000 Siberians sign decision cards to accept Christ.*"

In 1992, the *Book of Hope* came to the city of Krasnoyarsk in central Siberia — a city that had been under 70 years of communist atheism without a church. During six weeks of distributing the book in the schools during the day and inviting children to bring their parents to the hockey arena that seated 17,000 people for nightly rallies, we had 68,000 Siberians sign decision cards to accept Christ.

There was Olga. At birth, an alcoholic doctor made a terrible mistake, and Olga was born with a birth deformity that left one arm and leg twisted and all but useless. Children ridiculed her and Olga believed that nobody could ever love her. Then one day, a team came into her school and said, "We have a love letter. It's a letter from someone who loves you so much, He died to save you." Olga said her little 14-year-old heart beat rapidly, but her head said, "Nobody could ever love me." She took the book home, and as God's Word began to fill her heart, and her mind, and her life, a transformation took place. She was so excited she began to gather other children in her school so they could study the *Book of Hope* together. Today, that group of children has grown into a church of several thousand baptized believers in the city of Krasnoyarsk.

But Olga is not in Krasnoyarsk. God gave her a burden for the Muslim people, and she is today a missionary in a Muslim land, sent by a church that didn't exist in 1992. I'm talking about the incredible, indestructible power of this seed — God's Word.

Dima was there in Krasnoyarsk in 1992. A 17-year-old dedicated atheist, whose father was a member of the communist party. When the team came to his school with the book, he wasn't interested, but later some of the other students who had received the book asked him to come to the Hope Fest Celebration that night in the hockey arena.

In his own words, Dima testifies that as he heard "Bob Hoskins tell about Jesus" that word impacted his life and he found himself moving forward with hundreds of others to ask Jesus to come into his heart.

Dima started a Bible study with some young people and today that Bible study has also grown into a strong church in Krasnoyarsk, but Dima is not in Krasnoyarsk.

God gave him a burden for the lost of China. He went to Vladivostok in the Far East of Russia to study Chinese; while there he has planted a church and has several hundred members, but more importantly, it seems, he has opened an institute to train young Russian believers to be missionaries to China. Again, the incredible power of this indestructible seed — God's Word.

There are upwards of two thousand churches planted across those vast areas of the former Soviet Union, using the *Book of Hope* as their tool for evangelism. As we have been able to take God's Word to the children, and they have in turn shared it with their parents, it has transformed families, it has transformed communities, and they in turn are going to areas yet unreached to take this indestructible seed — God's Word.

Not only in El Salvador and Russia, but now around the world in more than 65 languages, this incorruptible and indestructible seed of God's Word is bringing forth a harvest in the most unlikely places, and in the most powerful way.

Living in one of the poorest sections of Nicaragua,

11-year-old Maria was trying to raise her three little brothers on her own. She woke up early every morning to make tortillas to sell on the street and to get her brothers ready for school. Then she spent most of her day trying to make enough money for them to survive.

She was tired, hungry and despairing. She realized she couldn't earn enough selling tortillas. She saw other girls selling their bodies as prostitutes and Maria decided she would rather die than do that. The latest rash of suicides gave Maria an idea. She decided to end the family's misery by killing her little brothers; then she would kill herself.

That same day, Maria's little brothers came home from school with the *Book of Hope*. After they begged Maria to read it to them, Maria began to read out loud about Jesus, who loved them so much that He had already paid the price for their sins!

Right then, she and her brothers prayed the prayer in the back of the book to receive Christ as Savior. They went to the church that had sent volunteers to their school with the *Book of Hope*, and they told the pastor of their decision to follow Jesus — and about their dire circumstances.

Today, that little girl and her brothers are receiving the support of their local church, and they are all vibrant new Christians. I'm talking about the power of God's Word!

Even in areas of the Muslim world this incorruptible seed is bringing forth a harvest. In Indonesia, the largest Muslim nation in the world, a *Book of Hope* volunteer named Cindy was on her way home from a full day of distribution. She stopped by the drugstore and was drawn to a young woman who looked very depressed. She noticed she had purchased a small bag of pills.

Cindy walked up to the girl and asked what was wrong. The girl, Marji, poured out a heart full of pain and anguish; she came from a broken home. It seems her friends had all deserted her. "I hate this life," she declared. She was ready to end it all; she planned to go home and take all the pills she had just bought.

"Wait, I have something for you," Cindy told her, and gave her the *Book of Hope*. Together they began to look through it and Cindy began to explain the love of Jesus from the book. "It can't be," Marji said. "Nobody loves me!"

But through the words of the book, and with Cindy's help, Marji accepted Christ's love and made a commitment right there to live her life for Jesus! The *Book of Hope*, God's Word, this indestructible seed helped save her life on the very day she had planned to commit suicide.

Today, by God's grace, the *Book of Hope* is being distributed in over 100 countries of the world. In June of 2004, we gave the 250 millionth copy of this indestructible seed to a beautiful girl named Delasi in the city of Ho, Ghana. Already we are hearing testimonies from Delasi and her family of the impact God's Word is having.

Now we see it really *is* possible — *God's Word. Every Child!*

# CHAPTER SIX

# God's Word

*"How can a young man keep his way pure? By living according to your word."*
**(Psalm 119:9)**

*"Oh, how I love your law! I meditate on it all day long."*
**(Psalm 119:97)**

*"Americans have the Bible but by and large they don't read it. And because they don't read it they have become a nation of Biblical illiterates."*
— George Gallup Jr. [1]

*"It takes about 71 hours to read the entire Bible at an average reading speed. With only 20 minutes a day you can read through the Bible approximately 1.5 times every year!"*
— Bob Hoskins

---

[1] *George Gallup Jr. and Jim Castelli. The Peoples Religion (NY McMillan Pub. Co. 1989).*

# 6

# God's Word

When Dr. Billy Graham conducted his first crusade in Great Britain, the response was so incredible he was invited to a meeting with Sir Winston Churchill. Sir Winston motioned for Dr. Graham to be seated and said, "Do you have any hope? What hope do you have for the world?" Billy took his New Testament, and from a perspective of God's Word answered, "Mr. Prime Minister, I'm filled with hope."

Sir Winston pointed at the early editions of three London newspapers and commented that they were filled with reports of rapes, murders and hate. He told Billy, "I am an old man and without hope for the world."

Billy replied, "Life is very exciting because I know what is going to happen in the future." Then he spoke about Jesus Christ, turning from place to place in the New Testament and explaining Christ's birth, death, resurrection, and the promise of the second coming of Christ.

At last Sir Winston said, "I do not see hope for the future unless it is this hope you are talking about; we must have a return to God."

Watching television newscasts today can be a depressing experience. Things have become even worse than they were when Billy Graham met with Winston Churchill. It seems that the news for the most part is invariably and inevitably bad. With war terrorists and a decline in values and morality, where will it all lead? Is there an answer? The answer for America and the world, I am convinced, is a revival of recognizing the place and importance of God's Word.

Staggering statistics reveal a decline in the place God's Word is given in American culture. Tragically, they also indicate a decline in the recognition of the importance of God's Word and the regular reading and study of God's Word among Christians. George Gallup Jr. is a pollster, who over the years has come to be trusted to provide accurate information on many topics, including what Americans know and believe about the Bible. For years they have kept a count on how much people read the Bible, how they understand it, and what they believe about it.

The 1938 Gallup Survey found the Bible was the most frequently encountered book on American bookshelves. The Bible was also the number one book in many surveys over the years. The tragedy then as now was the report of how few people actually read the Word of God. Also, of those who may have owned a Bible, but had doubts about its authenticity. Polls show that the proportion of Americans who believe the Bible is literally true fell by half in a quarter of a century. As recently as 1963, 65% of Americans believed the Bible was literally true. By 1978, this figure had fallen to 38%.

Polls today show that now just 12% think the Bible is the actual Word of God to be interpreted literally. The fact is that concurrent with the decline in moral values and the staggering consequences that this has brought our country, Americans no longer believe the Bible as they once did. They certainly do not read the Bible as they used to, and as a result they do not know and understand the Bible as they once did.

*Polls today show that now just 12% think the Bible is the actual Word of God to be interpreted literally.*

George Barna is another researcher who tracks trends as it relates to spiritual matters and moral questions. Reading through the Barna and Gallup research, you will discover that 25% of adults don't know that Easter celebrates the resurrection of Christ. Ten per cent of Americans believe that the Bible is an ancient book of fables, legends, history, and moral precepts. Only about 2 adults in 3 (64%) know that Jesus was born in Bethlehem.

Fewer than half of all adults can name Matthew, Mark, Luke, and John as the four Gospels of the New Testament, and again only 12% think the Bible should be interpreted literally. Staggering is the revelation of the lack of knowledge of the Bible among college graduates. Only 4 in 10 know that Jesus delivered the Sermon on the Mount. What is frightening is that many Christians are unaware of this dearth of Biblical knowledge.

Recently, we have seen success for books written by Christians. Some of these have become best sellers, even making the New York Times list, but it is not enough to read Christian books! It is not enough to read books about the Word of God. Christian books can never replace the consistent reading for ones self of God's Word.

Each of us needs to examine our habits as they relate to God's Word. There is a need to discipline ourselves and to regulate our lives so there will be time daily for careful, prayerful reading of the Word of God. If our lives are to reflect Christ, and if the Church is to have the influence in our world and on our culture as God intended it to have, then the Church must give priority to the Word of God.

It saddens me to see the decline in the corporate reading of God's Word in churches. Music, however beautiful; however inspiring; does not take the place of the sharing of God's Word corporately. There should be a time in every service when God's Word is read with emphasis upon all members not only listening but reading along with the public reading.

There was a time in American life when the family altar was a cornerstone. With the incredible speedup of our lives as a result of television, the Internet, and so many activities, the family altar is definitely in decline if not in most cases nonexistent.

I challenge young families to deliberately set a time and a place for the family to read God's Word together. It's wonderful if Dad reads, but each member of the family should be encouraged from time to time to be the reader. In times past, this was the mortar that often held families together — is it any wonder with the decline in family Bible-reading the staggering statistics of broken families continues to climb?

> *I challenge young families to deliberately set a time and a place for the family to read God's Word together.*

As driven home by the research of such credible people as George Barna and George Gallup Jr., it appears that many Americans who profess to be Christians have no personal relationship with Christ because of a lack of Biblical knowledge.

The reality of how one can be religious; make a profession; and have no personal experience with Christ is powerfully illustrated for me in the testimony of my dear and wonderful friend, Dr. Augustine Pinto.

Dr. Pinto, with his wife Grace and children, Snehal, Sonal, and Ryan lead, according to the Guinness Book of World Records, the largest private school system in the world. Over two hundred thousand students now attend the Ryan International Schools located in major cities of India.

The impact and the influence upon the lives of these hundreds of thousands of children is having an incredible affect upon India's future. Civil leaders, business leaders, and India's top entertainers made speeches during a sixtieth birthday celebration for Dr. Pinto in Mumbai, an event that extolled the success of both the man and the "school empire" he has established.

It is an amazing story of how he and Grace started 25 years ago in a rented garage, and today have reached a pinnacle of success never before achieved in the world of education. When Dr. Pinto was given an opportunity to respond to the many accolades that had been heaped upon him and his family, he began by saying, "Many ask what is the secret of the success?"

Dr. Pinto went on to explain his success, beginning with the fact that he began life as a devout Catholic who faithfully took communion and considered himself to be a "good Christian." At the same time, he said, his life was dominated by a desire for personal power and success. He had a driving ambition to succeed and to eventually enter politics and become a political leader in India.

Many of those who extolled his character virtues had remarked of the great love he had for the students attending his schools. They spoke of the emphasis placed upon building values and character within the lives of those children. Many went on to say that as a result of his passion for character development within the lives of the children, many of them would go on to transform India and impact its destiny. But Dr. Pinto, by his own confession, said that he had no interest in his students in those early days. He said he cared not about their character or their values. His driving ambition was to simply use the schools to create the financial capacity that would enable him to reach his personal goals and fulfill his carnal ambitions.

Eight years ago a member of his staff brought him a package as a birthday present.

"What is it?" Dr. Pinto inquired.

"It's a Bible," was the response.

"A Bible! What would I do with a Bible?" asked Dr. Pinto.

"Read it," said the staff member.

"But it's such a big book!" exclaimed Dr. Pinto. "Where would I begin reading?"

"I suggest you begin in the Gospel of John," said the staff member.

A few days later, Dr. Pinto picked up the gift Bible and finally found the Gospel of John. With a great deal of skepticism, he began to read. It had such an impact upon him that he read it the second time. His attention was especially drawn to the third chapter. It is the story of Nicodemus. He was struck by the words of Jesus to this spiritual leader within the Jewish community — a man trained in the law — a man who was supposedly leading others, and yet, Jesus said to him, "Nicodemus, you must be born again."

Dr. Pinto said these words pierced deep in his heart the realization that he was a religious man himself, but had never experienced this relationship that Christ described as being born again.

Over a period of time as Dr. Pinto read and studied God's Word, he made a personal decision, inviting Christ to take control of his life. He went to a local church and asked for water baptism.

In the meanwhile, God was at work in his wife, Grace, and the children. Within a matter of a year the entire family had experienced the beginning of a true relationship with Jesus Christ. Dr. Pinto shared this testimony with the hundreds assembled for his birthday celebration, and went on to say, "If there is any success in our lives and our family, it is because of our personal relationship with God through Jesus Christ." He took a great deal of time to ascribe all the glory and all the honor for the incredible success of the Ryan International Schools and the Pinto family businesses to his Lord and Savior, Jesus Christ.

Unfortunately many, like the Pintos, profess

Christianity but through a lack of understanding and knowledge of God's Word have not come to a personal, intimate, daily walk with Jesus Christ.

Do not be fooled into thinking you are a Christian because you go to church or were born into a "Christian family." The only way to be a Christian is to come into a personal relationship with Jesus Christ, let Him forgive your sins, and make walking with Him the priority in your life. The main key to the whole process is the Word of God, the Bible. Its power to transform cannot be overstated.

# CHAPTER SEVEN

# Doing *the* Impossible

*Jesus answered, "It is written: 'Man does not live on bread alone, but on every word that comes from the mouth of God.'"* (Matthew 4:4)

*"I have held many things in my hands and I have lost them all. But whatever I have placed in God's Hands that I still possess."*

— Martin Luther

# Doing *the* Impossible

I asked you earlier: Was Christ serious when He said to his disciples, His church, you and me, "go into all the world and preach the Gospel to every creature?" I'm sure we all realize that Christ would have never commanded the Church to do something impossible. I'm shocked to hear people say it is the impossible task. That there are just too many people in too many remote areas. That there are too many barriers: time, space, language. No, my friend, when Christ said go into all the world and give the Gospel to everybody, that is precisely what He intended for His Church, for you and me, to do. The thrilling fact is that never before has a generation had the opportunity that we have today.

Today, the Great Commission is far from fulfilled, for there are three billion people who have not yet had an adequate witness to the message that Jesus saves. But I believe the *Book of Hope* story proves that as a generation of believers becomes galvanized by the possibilities of this age and the power of God. We can be the ones who finally and faithfully carry the light to the ends of the earth. When we do, Christ has promised that we will usher in His triumphant return. When His disciples asked for a sign of His coming in Matthew 24, Jesus began by describing for them what life on earth would be like from His ascension till His return. He said:

> *Watch out that no one deceives you. For many will come in my name, claiming, 'I am the Christ,' and will deceive many. You will hear of wars and rumors of wars, but see to it that you are not alarmed. Such things must happen, but the end is still to come. Nation will rise against nation, and kingdom against kingdom. There will be famines and earthquakes in various places. All these are the beginning of birth pains.*
>
> *Then you will be handed over to be persecuted and put to death, and you will be hated by all nations because of me. At that time many will turn away from the faith and will betray and hate each other, and many false prophets will appear and deceive many people. Because of the increase of wickedness, the love of most will grow cold, but he who stands firm to the end will be saved.* (Matthew 24:4–13)

It's easy to understand this is not a list of specific signs for, obviously, all the things Christ lists have been happening for 2,000 years. Furthermore, the disciples had not asked for signs, plural, but for a sign, singular. It is in verse 14 that Jesus answers their question and gives THE SIGN of His return *"and this Gospel of the Kingdom shall be preached in the whole world as a testimony to all the nations, and then the end will come."*

I know what some of you are asking yourselves even now, "But what can I do? I'm not an evangelist, a preacher. I'm probably too shy to even speak publicly about my faith, so what can I do?"

The powerful truth is outlined for us by Jesus in Mark chapter four. It is that incredible chapter where He talks about sowing and reaping; where He talks about planting and harvest. He talks about seed falling on various kinds of soil. The heart of that chapter is Christ's undeniable revelation that the power is not in the *sower;* the power is in the *seed.*

It is clear in this chapter that the seed is the Word of God. Christ's teachings, as well as nature, make it clear that the seed has a power and life of its own. That seed need only be sown or planted, and without the sower even understanding how it works, the power of the seed begins to produce.

Jesus powerfully illustrates it when He speaks of the farmer *scattering* the seed, and then he goes about his daily routine. Jesus says, night and day, whether he sleeps or gets up, that seed is sprouting and growing, even though it is a mystery to the sower.

Sometimes we act like God asked us to do things

which He did not. Sometimes we suppose that it is our responsibility to go out into the world to convict people, to convince people, even to convert people — and, of course, we exclaim, "Impossible! I can't do that!" And, of course, we cannot do that. Convicting, convincing, converting, this is the sovereign work of God's Holy Spirit, but the undeniable truth found in God's Word is that He has appointed us, His church, His disciples, to be the proclaimers. The Bible speaks of preaching the Word, publishing the Word, and in Christ's parable, scattering the Word, the indestructible seed.

> "... if we will scatter the Word, God declares by Himself ... that His Word will never return void or empty."

When we proclaim, when we publish, when we scatter this seed, it is the work of the Holy Spirit, in some way mysterious to us, to speak to the human heart and the act of producing results is the act of the Holy Spirit.

God has pledged Himself to His Word. He spoke to the prophet Isaiah in chapter 55, verse 11, and again proclaims that if we will preach the Word; if we will publish the Word; if we will scatter the Word, God declares by Himself, by the mighty power with which He flung the cosmos into existence, that His Word will never return void or empty. Rather He says, it will accomplish the eternal purpose for which He has sent it. We are always inclined to think the power is in the sower. We hear a great Bible teacher, or we listen to a powerful evangelist, and we are convinced that they are people of great power. Traveling around the world, after the fall of the TV evangelist, Jimmy Swaggart, I met people in country after country — Hindus, even Muslims — who testified to accepting Christ as a result of watching Jimmy Swaggart on television or listening to one of his video sermons. And I ask again and again, how can it be that a man who is living an immoral life can see such results from his preaching?

Perhaps this is what Jesus was speaking to when he said, *"Many will say to me on that day, 'Lord, Lord, did we not prophesy in your name, and in your name drive out demons and perform many miracles?' Then I will tell them plainly, 'I never knew you. Away from me, you evildoers!'"* (Matthew 7:22–23). Swaggart was proclaiming the truth as it relates to salvation. He was scattering the seed of God's Word, and though he himself might not have been living righteously, the seed that is scattered does not understand that; it has a power and a life of its own, and when it reaches the soil, when it touches the human heart, Jesus said it would produce a harvest.

This is true even if the proclaimer is the most godly and most righteous man that you may know. The result does not come because of his personal righteousness, the result comes because the power is in the seed that is scattered.

Isn't that incredible? It means that no one is excluded; no one is left out, that all of us who have received Jesus Christ can be scatterers of seed. It may be the simple act of handing someone a Scripture portion or of quoting some passage from God's Word, and that seed will touch the human spirit and change the heart.

Now, don't be discouraged if you do not see the immediate harvest of the seeds you sow. I have heard that for an adult to come to Christ, it usually takes a series of 9 or 10 events or exposures to the Gospel ... so when you quote a verse to a struggling friend, and he doesn't respond by wanting to pray the sinner's prayer with you, don't worry. You might be seed number four, or seed number eight, and somewhere down the line, seed planter number ten will seal the deal in God's timing. That's okay. The Apostle Paul told the Corinthian church that all who preached to them had a hand in their salvation, but it was God Who saved them ... *"I planted the seed, Apollos watered it, but God made it grow."* (1 Corinthians 3:6).

CHAPTER EIGHT

# The Mission

*"For the word of God is living and active. Sharper than any double-edged sword, it penetrates even to dividing soul and spirit, joints and marrow; it judges the thoughts and attitudes of the heart."*
(Hebrews 4:12)

# *The* Mission

Best-selling Christian author Randy Alcorn has amended the adage "you can't take it with you," with this counterpart: "but you can send it on ahead." Your treasures on earth will stay on earth when you go home to be with Jesus ... but the treasures you have invested in the kingdom will be there waiting for you.

When we saw how the *Book of Hope* could reach millions of students with God's Word, right in their public school classrooms, all around the world, we knew this was our calling. And God gave the *Book of Hope* ministry this simple mission:

"To affect destiny by providing God's eternal Word to all the children and youth of the world."

Then, as we determined to keep our hearts and hands clean before Him and listen for His leading, God began to open the doors. Russia and Eastern Europe, Latin America and the Caribbean, even Asia and the Pacific Rim — India, the Philippines, Thailand, and now Cambodia and even Vietnam. The churches of China are anxious for us to somehow get the *Book of Hope* to their students, and even some youngsters in the Middle East are now receiving it.

The plan is very simple, too. Local churches organize to carry the *Book of Hope* into the schools, with the permission of local school boards and government. They present the book and share its message in classrooms and school assemblies, and they usually invite the students to a Hope Fest Celebration concert, where they hear good music and experience drama and Bible teachings. The results are wonderful, as children, youth and whole families are saved and grounded in a local church.

People often exclaim over the *Book of Hope*, for the miracle that it takes just 33¢ to put the *Book of Hope* into the hand of a child, and yet the results around the world go beyond human imagination: families transformed, villages changed, churches planted. We shouldn't be surprised, because in Mark chapter four, Jesus talks about the grain of mustard seed, so small, yet when it is planted into the soil, it grows into a great plant larger than all others. For the power is never in the sower; the power is always in the seed.

Today, each and every one of us has the opportunity to obey Christ's command and to reach the world by planting this indestructible seed. God is calling you to be a part of this community that takes seriously His command to preach the gospel in every nation and to fulfill the great commission in our generation. Let there be no misunderstanding. No one is excluded; all who have received God's mercy and grace are commissioned by our Lord to be seed scatterers. The Scripture is very clear, if we do not go, the lost will never hear. There can be no misunderstanding about this, for God spoke and said, *"When I say to the wicked man, 'you will surely die,' and you do not warn him or speak out to dissuade him from his evil ways in order to save his life, that wicked man will die for his sin, and I will hold you accountable for his blood."* (Ezekiel 3:18)

Today, as never before we have the opportunity to go with the Good News. We have been entrusted with this indestructible seed, and today there are multiple opportunities allowing us to be participants in the last day harvest.

One way that you can be a part of this great mission is through your prayers, and I plead with you to pray every day for the children. We are experiencing increasing spiritual warfare. It is only through your prayers and God's faithfulness that we continue to move forward, proclaiming the Good News.

Colossians 4:2-3 makes my plea, *"Devote yourselves to prayer, being watchful and thankful. And pray for us, too, that God may open a door for our message, so that we may proclaim the mystery of Christ."* The prayers of friends like you open the doors for the gospel, pave the way for our Affect Destiny Teams, saturate our Hope

Fest Celebrations and distributions with God's Spirit, and insure the safety of our staff and volunteers. You bring down the strongholds of Satan when you lift us up in your prayers!

In addition to your prayers, I invite you to give. The means to reach the next generation around the world is in our hands today. The *Book of Hope* is a cost effective tool for telling children and families everywhere about Jesus. The miracle is that it takes just 33¢ to place the *Book of Hope* into the hands of a needy child or youth. Every dollar you give reaches three students with the *Book of Hope*. Where else can your dollars go so far toward world evangelism? And when we sow the seed of God's Word into such fertile ground, we reap a great harvest of souls. Most Christians (80% or more) say they received Christ as Savior before the age of 18. Youngsters are the most tenderhearted segment of the population, open to the truth of the Gospel. Your investment in telling children about Jesus is wise and will produce eternal benefits.

> *"Every dollar you give reaches three students with the Book of Hope. Where else can your dollars go so far toward world evangelism?"*

One way that your prayers and giving can be most effective is through the CLUB 365 outreach. This dynamic program allows you to give God's Word to three school children every single day of the year.

When you make a CLUB 365 commitment, you will be reaching young people like Maxim from Chernigov, Ukraine. Like some sullen teenagers, Maxim was quarrelsome and rebellious. His mother feared he would follow in the footsteps of his dad and become an alcoholic. In this despairing nation, what could change that path? The Gospel of Jesus could!

Maxim read the *Book of Hope* and now he is a believer — as well as being the church pianist. He has led his sister to the Lord and is praying for his parents' salvation. Their church was started through *Book of Hope* outreach in their city of Chernigov.

You will give the *Book of Hope* to a boy like Artuom from Magnitogorsk, Russia. His mom is a follower of Hare Krishna and his father is an atheist. What hope does he have for eternity? The hope of Jesus, delivered in the *Book of Hope*! He received the *Book of Hope* at school and today, he is a committed believer, sings in the youth choir, helps to lead his church youth group and witnesses to his friends!

(Oh, yes — the church Artuom attends was also launched through the *Book of Hope* in Artuom's home city of Magnitogorsk.)

You can also give the *Book of Hope* to a young lady

like Irina, who lives with her six brothers and sisters in a gypsy village on the outskirts of Minsk, Belarus. With the severe economic struggles in the former Soviet Union, what hope is there for Irina's future? There's the eternal hope of Jesus. She received the *Book of Hope* in school, and now she is a vibrant Christian — telling her friends about Jesus and helping translate English teaching materials into Russian for her church.

When you become a CLUB 365 member, you put the *Book of Hope* into the hands of three students like these all over the former Soviet Union, Latin America, Eastern Europe, Africa, Asia and around the world, every single day! Your commitment of just $1 a day reaches three youngsters like these, each and every day!

I realize giving $1 a day works out to $30 a month, $365 a year, and that is a sacrificial commitment for many people. But I boldly ask for it because of the children I've met who are still waiting to receive the hope of the Gospel.

I think of Nina, a Bosnian girl forced into a refugee camp with her sister and grandma. Their parents stayed behind to try to save their home, but their dad was executed by the advancing enemy.

I want to give hope to children like Nina, and I trust that you want to help, too, I believe someday we'll meet Nina in heaven and she will say, "Thank you for caring enough to give, so I could meet Jesus!"

That's not just wishful thinking. I have met so

many young people whose lives of hatred and bitterness have been completely, miraculously transformed by the power of God's Word.

I think of Sondra, a 22-year-old Muslim woman whose father, like Nina's, was killed in the Bosnian conflict. Sondra grew up angry and afraid, consumed by hatred for those who had murdered her father and so many of her friends. But some friends cared enough to pass along the Scriptures and today Sondra's heart is filled with courage, faith, and an incredible love for those whose fury cost her so dearly.

Today, Sondra says that if she sees the man who killed her father, "I will hug him, and tell him Jesus loves him."

Sondra's mother and one of her sisters have also accepted Christ; she is praying that her two other sisters will believe one day, too. They are among the millions who still haven't met Him ... but every day you can tell three youngsters the Good News with your commitment of $1 a day as a member of CLUB 365. For more information on this exciting outreach, please call toll-free 1-800-GIV-BIBL (448-2425) or return the coupon in the back of this book with your first month's commitment. It will make an eternal difference to three children in need, every single day.

Let me tell you about other ways you can scatter seed and be a member of CLUB 365 by going and personally placing God's Word into the hands of a student.

Book of Hope Affect Destiny Teams are the "going" arm of Book of Hope. It is our mission to reach every child with God's Word. We enable national believers like you to cross continents and personally deliver God's Word — in the form of the *Book of Hope* — to a student that may have never heard the Gospel before. You get to work with the local church to bring the salvation story to life through drama, songs, testimonies and citywide evangelistic crusades called "HopeFests."

*"You have the opportunity to go with the Gospel. The incredible power of mass media makes it possible."*

Teams range from ten day to four months and leave throughout the year. You can even join our Response Team for one to two years and be a part of the behind-the-scenes training and opening of new countries. For more information, call our offices (800-448-2425) or visit our Web site www.bookofhope.net

Today, as never before, the Church has the opportunity to go with the Gospel. You have the opportunity to go with the Gospel. The incredible power of mass media makes it possible.

For the most part, in this book, I have been speaking about the power of the printed Word. I have been a literature missionary for more than 30 of my 50 years in missions.  By God's grace I have participated in the production and distribution of multiplied millions of copies of the printed Word.

Several years ago, I received a letter from a missionary in Madagascar.  He thanked me for the *Book of Hope* and gave exciting testimony of its impact on the children in the schools in Madagascar.  Then he asked a question which stabbed me to my innermost being.  He said, "Brother Bob, more than 40% of the children in Madagascar cannot read.  We cannot reach them with the book.  How are we to tell them Jesus' story."

For days I pondered this question.  I consulted with my son Rob.  We did some research to discover that there are many that will not be reached with the printed page.  We identified four groups that will never be touched, for the most part, by our printed *Book of Hope*.  There are the illiterates, that percentage of 32% no matter how beautiful the book, it cannot affect them.  There are those we call pre-literate, children who are in school, often in third world countries, but the reading comprehension is not high enough to fully understand scripture until they are perhaps ten or eleven years of age.  By then in today's world, Satan has already impacted them with the evils and the immoralities — they need to hear Jesus' story long before.

There are then the aliterates.  The aliterates are those who live in the United States, Western Europe and major capitals of the world, who can read but for the most part don't read. Today, their media preference is not a book, but the Internet, the computer, video, the silver screen. Finally, there are those we refer to as inaccessible countries, for example China, where we will be able to distribute, by God's grace, millions of books, but there are over 400 million students, and if we are going to fulfill our mission to get Christ's story to every child and youth in the world, we must have some other medium to touch these masses in an inaccessible area.

As Rob and I began to pray and seek God through His grace, He brought to us experts in the field of mass communication to children and young people, people who had produced television series for major networks who were among the elite of Hollywood. In God's providence we found believers among them, and as we partnered among them, we have been able to produce the animated, photo-realistic, cutting-edge movie based on the *Book of Hope* story.

If you would like to know more about other powerful tools we are using to reach the lost children of the world check online or at the back of this book for information about our online outreach to teenagers (www.hopenet.net) and the new animated version of the *Book of Hope*, the movie *The GodMan*.

Now is the acceptable time. Today is the day of salvation. People have tried to bury and discount God's indestructible seed for centuries, and yet when we scatter it under the sun, it still blossoms into an incredible harvest for the Lord. You don't have to be an evangelist to proclaim the Word. You can join with the *Book of Hope* ministry today, and be part of reaching millions of children and youth with the Gospel — and be part of fulfilling the Great Commission, in your own lifetime! You can be part of the immense vision ... *God's Word. Every Child!*

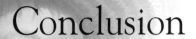

# Conclusion

Down through history, God has used the written Word to give His message to the world. Some day the task of world evangelism will be completed, and the end time events recorded in the book of Revelation will be played out. I am awed to realize the importance of books in all of these end time events.

*"And he had in his hand a little book open"* (Revelation 10:2). When the mighty angel appeared in the vision of John, the main instrument of his power was the little book. He was clothed with a cloud. He wore a rainbow on his head. His face was shining like the sun because he was a bearer of light. He stood ready for the widest usefulness, his right foot upon the land and his left foot upon the sea. In his hand, as the main instrument of his power, he held *"a little book open."* Think of it! When the angel comes to *"swore by him that liveth forever and ever, who created heaven, and the things that therein are, and the earth, and the things that therein are, and the sea, and the things which are therein, that there should be time no longer"* (Revelation 10:6), he will not come with a sword of military conquest. He will not come with the methods of world commerce. He will not come with some great ecclesiastical system. But in his

hand he will hold a little book!

Again, in John's vision, the seer records that he *"saw the dead, small and great, stand before God; and the books were opened: and another book was opened, which is the book of life; and the dead were judged out of those things which were written in the books, according to their works"* (Revelation 20:12). John goes on to declare that the sea, death, and hell deliver up the dead which are in them. Finally, death and hell are cast into the lake of fire.

But the words that ring in my heart as we face the challenge of the unfinished task of the Great Commission are found in the final verse of chapter 20: *"And whosoever was not found written in the book of hope was cast into the lake of fire"* (verse 15).

I am one hundred per cent convinced that through mass distribution of the book God has placed in our hands, we can snatch millions from the burning fire, who will rise up on that judgment day and call us blessed.

Perhaps you have experienced the power of God's Word in your own life. We would love to hear your story. Please go online today at www.indestructibleseed.net and post your testimony. You can tell the world that you know, from the change in your own life, that the seed of the Word is the power of God to salvation!

The field is the world. The seed is the Word. He has entrusted the seed to us. We are the sowers. It is the Spirit of God that causes that seed to multiply. In Mark chapter four, Jesus told several stories that each ended with fantastic growth, with harvest time, with a "harvest beyond their wildest dreams." One of the stories ended with the tree so tall, strong and sturdy, that eagles could make their nest in it. One of the stories ended with a beacon of light set high on a lamp stand drawing all those in darkness to it.

The end of our story is in Revelation 22 at the gates of the heavenly city where the crystal river runs from the throne of God and a tree bears fruit for the healing of the nations, with Christ as the light of that city, who says, *"I am Jesus! And I am the one who sent the angel to tell you of all these things for the churches. I am David's Great Descendent and I am also the bright morning star. The Spirit and bride say, 'Come!' Everyone who hears this should say, 'Come!' If you are thirsty, come! If you want life-giving water, come and take it. It's free."* (Revelation 22:16–17).

Jesus is calling to the lost, but so are you and me: "The Spirit and the Bride say, 'Come!'" The Church is the Bride of Christ, and with our beloved Savior we call to the lost to come to new life in Him. Call out the Good News today. Spread the indestructible seed for all the children and youth of the world.

*God's Word. Every Child.*

# How has the power of God's Word transformed your life?

## www.indestructibleseed.net

Go to our website today, and post your personal story
of how the Word of God impacted you.

**God has promised:**
*"So is my word that goes out from my mouth: It will not
return to me empty, but will accomplish what I desire
and achieve the purpose for which I sent it"*
(Isaiah 55:11).

We believe that the Word of God is never sown in vain,
and that its seeds have the power to transform hearts
and lives, wherever they are planted.

Your story will build that same faith
in others — share it today!

Visit www.indestructibleseed.net
and post your testimony.

# www.hopenet.net
## for teens

Recent statistics say one of the most common uses people have for the Internet is to search for spiritual direction online!

While there are many great church websites, there are relatively few designed for *unchurched* teenagers who may be looking for hope.

Our www.hopenet.net presents the entire text of the youth version *Book of Hope,* but there is much more: testimony stories of other teenagers, an interactive game, chat rooms with "cyber missionary" teenagers who offer advice and guidance and much more. Steer all teenagers to www.hopenet.net.

# The GodMan

## The animated *Book of Hope*

Due for a 2005 debut, *The GodMan* was created by top Hollywood filmmakers with the latest computer generated

animation for a powerful re-telling of the life story of Jesus.

This film is the Word of God for Third World youngsters who can't or choose not to read — with exciting special effects, great music and a clear salvation story. *The GodMan* can even go into restricted areas where the printed *Book of Hope* is not yet welcome.

Find out more at www.bookofhope.net!

# *G*et *involved!*

## Take an Affect Destiny Team Mission this year!

Spend a week or more overseas with the *Book of Hope!*

You will take the book into schools, share your testimony with children and distribute God's Word, be part of Hope Fest Celebration concerts, and much more!

You can bring a whole group from your church, or join an existing team yourself. Affect Destiny Teams are leaving about every other week throughout the school year, to join with local believers and get the Word to the children and youth!

You may join a team bound for Latin America, the Caribbean, Eastern Europe, Russia, India or beyond!

Call Vanessa Mitchell, write or visit online for more details!

**www.bookofhope.net • 1.800.GIV.BIBL (448.2425)**
*Book of Hope • 3111 SW 10th Street • Pompano, Florida 33069*

# Just 33¢

## made a life-transforming difference!

In Scotland, Kirsty's mom was a single parent with two teenaged girls to raise, and it wasn't easy. In fact, Kirsty and her friends were at that stage where they wanted to dress in revealing clothes, put on lots of makeup and dance all night at rock concerts. But when a *Book of Hope* Affect Destiny Team invited them to a Gospel concert at a Hope Fest Celebration, everything changed. Today Kirsty, her sister and her mother are all following Jesus!

Imagine — it took just 33¢ to reach Kirsty with the *Book of Hope* and transform her life ... and similar stories are being told in 100 nations around the world, as students are receiving the *Book of Hope* today. You can help, through your prayers, and through a gift. Every dollar reaches three students with the message of salvation.

-------------------------------------------------------------------------

## Book of Hope

☐ Please tell me how I can get involved in the *Book of Hope* ministry.

☐ Please send me the following free gift (please mark **one**):
    ☐ *Affect Destiny: The Book of Hope Story.*
    ☐ *Then: Seeds of Spiritual Lineage*
    ☐ *250 Millionth Distribution DVD*

☐ I have enclosed
    ☐ first monthly gift of $30
    ☐ annual gift of $365 as a member of CLUB 365, to reach three students every single day!

☐ I have enclosed a gift, I understand every dollar reaches three children and youth with the *Book of Hope*

*over* >>>

# Club 365
## lets you tell three students
## about Jesus, every single day!

Give your first monthly gift of $30, and pledge to give $1 per day

— and you will reach three children or youth with the

*Book of Hope* every single day of the year!

Just mark the box below to become a member of Club 365 today!

www.bookofhope.net • 1.800.GIV.BIBL (448.2425)
Book of Hope • 3111 SW 10th Street • Pompano, Florida 33069

- - - - - - - - - - - - - - - - - - - - - - - - - - - - - - - - - - - - - - - - - - - - - - - - -

☐ $100 to reach 300 students
☐ $50 to reach 150 students
☐ $25 to reach 75 students
☐ $_____ to help as much as possible

NAME

ADDRESS

CITY                                              STATE        ZIP

PHONE   (            )

E-MAIL                        @

Return to Book of Hope • 3111 SW 10th Street • Pompano, Florida 33069.
**1.800.GIV.BIBL (448.2425) • www.bookofhope.net**

# Exciting video direct from India

Discover the power of
God's Word to transform!

## See with your own eyes

God's power to transform lives through His
Word — even in the heart of darkness!

For two thousand years, India has been
enslaved to demonism through the pantheon
of Hindu god and goddesses still followed by
some 80% of the people ...

... but when the national believers began using the *Book of
Hope*, to reach children in their schools with the Word of
God, there were miraculous changes!

In this video, you will witness the transforming
power of the Word, especially in the life of nine-
year-old Jony, and his father, who had been all but
paralyzed by severe arthritis.

Discover this powerful truth, and share
it with your church. Send for the India
DVD today.

www.bookofhope.net
1.800.GIV.BIBL (448.2425)
*Book of Hope • 3111 SW 10th Street
• Pompano, Florida 33069*

# Affect Destiny:
## The Book of Hope Story

Call, write or go online to request the powerful book that tells the history of the *Book of Hope* ministry — and builds your faith with exciting true stories of dozens of lives that have been transformed!

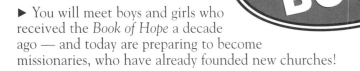

▶ You will meet boys and girls who received the *Book of Hope* a decade ago — and today are preparing to become missionaries, who have already founded new churches!

▶ You will listen to Jesus' parables from Mark chapter four with a new ear for His "stories" that spoke intimately to the hearts of His listeners — and see how His method of teaching the most important truths still works today.

▶ You will discover how two important women from the Bible — Mary and Esther — illustrate our calling as Christians in these final days of human history, a critical time that is both dangerous and thrilling.

▶ And you will find yourself caught up in a God-given plan to reach an entire generation with the Word, a plan that is do-able and is being done right now!

Call, write or visit us online and request *Affect Destiny: The Book of Hope Story*

**www.bookofhope.net**
**1.800.GIV.BIBL (448.2425)**
*Book of Hope • 3111 SW 10th Street*
*• Pompano, Florida 33069*

# Then: Seeds of Spiritual Lineage

## By Rob Hoskins

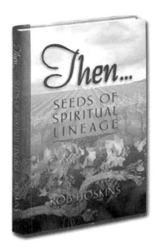

Book of Hope Executive Director Rob Hoskins presents an important look at the promises of Jesus in John chapters 14–16, such as:

**"I will do whatever you ask" (John 14:13).**
**"Pray for whatever you want, and your prayers will be answered" (John 15:7).**
**"The Father will give you whatever you ask for in my name" (John 15:16).**

Was Jesus telling the truth? And if so, why do so many of our prayers go unanswered? In *Then: Seeds of Spiritual Lineage*, Rob Hoskins shows that the promises of Christ were prefaced with a command that must be obeyed in order to receive the answers you seek.

"I have discovered that when we fulfill the IF before the THEN in Jesus' promises, He can answer our prayers and use our obedience to create a spiritual lineage from our works — a lineage that you may never even realize has followed you on this earth," Hoskins says.

Discover the truth about Christ's promises of overwhelming abundance, and why He would make such promises in the first place. Call, write or visit online to request *Then: Seeds of Spiritual Lineage*.

**www.bookofhope.net • 1.800.GIV.BIBL (448.2425)**
*Book of Hope • 3111 SW 10th Street • Pompano, Florida 33069*